Bradwell

BOOK OF

Wit & Hu

THE BRITS
UP NORTH

IVOR BUTLER
POKES FUN AT HIS FRIENDS UP NORTH

BRADWELL
BOOKS

Published by Bradwell Books

9 Orgreave Close Sheffield S13 9NP

Email: books@bradwellbooks.co.uk

Compiled by Ivor Butler

British Library Cataloguing in Publication Data: a catalogue record for this book is available from the British Library.

1st Edition

ISBN: 9781910551288

Design & Typeset by: Jenks Design

Illustrations: ©Tim O'Brien 2016

Back cover cartoon: © Chris Horlock 2016

Print: Hobbs the Printers, Totton Hants

"Northerners think they have the monopoly on beautiful scenery, open-hearted friendliness, honesty, sportsmanship and good beer; they were right about the scenery." A Southerner

A Scouser went to the doctor's.

"I think I'm a kleptomaniac, doc," he says, "Can you help me?"

"Take these pills," says the GP, "and if they don't work in two weeks, get me a flat screen telly."

Q: What do you call a Scouser in a suit?
A: The accused.

A Man U fan appeared in court one day charged with disorderly conduct and assault. The arresting officer stated that the accused had thrown something into the river.

"What exactly did the accused throw?" the judge asked. "Stones, sir," replied the police officer.

"Well, that's hardly an offence is it?" said the judge irritably.

"It was in this case, sir," said the officer, "Stones was the referee."

Q: How can you tell when a Scouser is lying?
A: His lips are moving.

Derby County were playing Charlton when the Derby County centre-forward took a knock to the head and was laid out on the pitch. His manager came running over just as the player regained consciousness.

"He doesn't know his own name," said the medic, "He's got no idea who he is."

"That's okay," said the manager, "Tell him he's Pele and send him back on."

The rivalry between Celtic and Rangers in Scotland is well known. A Celtic fan, looking for trouble, went up to a complete stranger in Glasgow and yelled, "To hell with Rangers!"

The stranger gave him a funny look and replied, "I don't know what you're talking about, mate. I'm from London. England!"

The Celtic fan was taken back for a moment, but then his face lit up and he yelled, "To hell with Queen's Park Rangers then!"

Northern man to his mate from the south: "I've got a really bad back."

His mate "You wanna support Blackburn Rovers – they've got four of 'em.

A Londoner walks into a bank in Oldham and says to the female assistant at the counter, "I want to open a current account now!"

The lady replied, "I beg your pardon, sir, what did you say?"

"Listen cloth-ears," snapped the man aggressively, "I said I want to open a current account right now!"

"Sir, I'm sorry," said the flustered assistant, "but we do not tolerate rudeness to staff in this bank."

The assistant left the window, went over to the bank manager and complained to him about her customer. They both returned and the manager spoke sternly to the aggressive customer, "What seems to be the problem here?"

"There's no problem," the Londoner said, "I just won 50 million in the lottery and I want to open a current account in this bank right now!"

"I see, sir," the manager said, "and this silly woman is giving you a hard time, is she?"

A Liverpudlian man walked into a Private Investigator's Office in London holding a pencil and a piece of very thin paper.

"I want you to trace someone for me," he said to the private eye.

A bus load of tourists from Leicester arrives in Windsor. The northerners gather around the guide who tells them, "This is the spot, here at Runnymede, where King John signed the Magna Carta."

A fellow at the front of the crowd asks, "When did that happen, lad?"

"1215," answers the guide.

The man looks at his watch and says, "Damn! Just missed it by a half hour!"

A man and his wife were sitting in their living room in Whitehaven and he said to her, "Just so you know, pet, I never want to live in a vegetative state, dependent on some machine and fluids from a bottle. If that ever happens, just pull the plug."

His wife got up, unplugged the TV and threw out all of his beer.

In a remote convent on the Northumbrian coast, the 98-year-old Mother Superior lay dying. The nuns gathered around her bed, trying to make her last days comfortable. They gave her some fresh warm milk to drink from their own dairy cow. She turned her face away, refusing to drink it.

One of the nuns took the glass back to the kitchen and she remembered that the previous Christmas a grateful visitor had given the convent a bottle of single-malt whisky. She opened it and poured a generous amount into the warm milk. Back at Mother Superior's bed, she held the glass to her lips. The old nun drank a little, then a little more and before they knew it she had drunk the whole glass down to the last drop.

"Mother," the nuns asked earnestly, "please give us some wisdom before you die."

The Mother Superior raised herself up in bed and, with a pious look on her face, said, "Don't sell that cow!"

Yorkshireman: "I'm thinking and I 'ave a question for yer – why have women niver bin t' moon?"

His mate: "I don't rightly know. Why have women niver bin t' moon?"

Yorkshireman: "Because it niver needed cleaning."

Q: What do you say to a graduate from the University of Huddersfield?

A: I'll have fries with that.

There were three escaped convicts - two cockneys and a Cumbrian – on the run from the police. With the police right on their tails, the convicts run into a forest and decide to climb up trees to hide. The police run into the forest in hot pursuit, only to lose track of the convicts. Suddenly, one of the officers looks up and sees a shadow in the trees. He alerts the other officers and asks, "What's that up in the tree?"

The cockney convict thinks quickly and replies, "Twit-o-woooo!" The officer says, "Aw, it's only an owl."

They walk on but they spot another shadow in a nearby tree and stop.

The other cockney convict, thinking his mate had the right idea, and goes, "Meowwww!"

The cop says, "Oh there's some poor cat stuck up there."

After another few minutes, the eagle-eyed officer sees the third convict and confers with his fellow officers. The Cumbrian convict decides to try the same method as his pals to fool the police below him.

He takes a deep breath and bellows at the top of his lungs, "Mooooooo!"

Q: What's a Geordie's idea of a balanced diet?
A: A bottle of brown in each hand.

At a match between Leeds United and Milton Keynes Dons, a Leeds fan found himself in the thick of dozens of flying bottles.

"There's nothing to worry about, mate," said the elderly chap standing next to him. "It's like the bombs during the war. You won't get hit unless the bottle's got your name on it."

"That's just what I'm worried about," said the Leeds fan, "my name's John Smith."

Q: What's the difference between Stoke City and a cocktail stick?

A: A cocktail stick has two points.

A Geordie moves to Watford and applies for a job as a handyman.

At the interview, his future boss asks, "Can you do electrics, son?"

"Oh no, man," says the Geordie.

"But you can do carpentry?" says the governor.

"No, man, no carpentry," says the Geordie.

"Well, how about plumbing then?" the guv asks, getting a bit tetchy.

"Oh, no, man," says the Geordie, "I divvint know owt about plumbing."

"You're not very handy then, are you?" says the boss.

"Aye, of course I am, man," says the Geordie, "I live round the corner."

Apparently, the Bolton manager offered to send the squad on an all-expenses paid holiday to Florida, but they said they'd rather go to Blackpool so they could see what it's like to ride on an open-top bus.

Q: What's the difference between a Yorkshire man and a coconut?
A: One's thick and hairy, and the other's a tropical fruit.

Little Brad in Brighton phones his uncle in Lincolnshire and says, "Thanks for the harmonica you gave me for my birthday. It's the best present I ever got."

"That's great," said his uncle. "So you know how to play it well then?"

"Oh, I don't play it," little Brad replied. "My mum gives me a fiver a week not to play it during the day, and my dad gives me a fiver a week not to play it at night!"

A glamorous woman from Altrincham was out shopping in the Blue Water Shopping Centre when she was accosted by a dirty, shabby-looking homeless woman who asked her for a couple of pounds for food.

The woman took out her purse, extracted ten pounds and asked, "If I give you this money, will you buy some wine with it instead of food?"

"No, I had to stop drinking years ago," the homeless woman replied somewhat surprised.

"Will you use it to go clothes shopping instead of buying food?" the woman asked.

"No, I don't waste time shopping," the homeless woman said. "I need to spend all my time trying to stay alive."

"Will you spend it at a beauty salon then instead of buying food?" the woman asked.

"Are you NUTS?!" exclaimed the homeless woman. "I haven't had my hair done in twenty years!"

"Well," said the woman, "I'm not going to give you the money. Instead, I'm going to take you out for dinner with my hubby and myself tonight."

The homeless woman was astounded. "Won't your husband be furious with you for doing that?" she asked, "I know I'm dirty, and I probably smell pretty disgusting."

"That's okay," replied the woman from Altrincham, "It's important for him to see what a woman looks like after she has given up shopping, hair appointments and wine."

A Mancunian and his lass Sharon are walking along Piccadilly one night. She sees a necklace in a window of a jewellers and says, "Oh, Darren, I'd love that!" so Darren throws a brick through the window and gives her the necklace.

A bit further down, she sees a handbag in a clothes shop window and says, "Oh, Darren, I'd REALLY love that!" so Darren throws a brick through the window of the shop and hands her the handbag.

Further along she stops outside a shoe shop and says, "Ooh, Darren I'd REALLY REALLY love those!" and Darren says, "What's the matter with you Sharon, do you think I'm made of bricks?"

In a fish and chip shop in Blackpool, a Surrey man is waiting for his meal. The woman behind the counter says, "I'm sorry for the delay with your order, dear. It should be with you shortly."

The Surrey man replies, "That's okay, love, but if you don't mind me asking, what sort of bait are you using?"

Q: Why should you never ask a person if they come from Yorkshire?
A: Because if they are not from Yorkshire, they'll be insulted. And if they are from Yorkshire, they'd have told you already.

A cockney is up in Manchester for a weekend when has a heart attack and is taken to the Royal Infirmary. The doctor tells him that he will not live unless he has a heart transplant right away. Another doctor runs into the room and says, "You're in luck, two hearts just became available, so you will get to choose which one you want. One belonged to one of the best lawyers in Manchester and one belonged to one of the most dedicated social workers."

Quick as a flash the cockney says, "Give me the lawyer's, mate." The doctor says, "Wait! Don't you want to know a little about them before you make your decision?"

The cockney says, "I already know enough, mate. We all know that social workers are bleeding hearts and the lawyer's probably never used his. So I'll take the lawyer's!"

A party of northerners are walking on Exmoor. After several hours they became hopelessly lost. One of them studied the map for some time, turning it this way and that, up and down, identifying distant landmarks, consulting his compass, noting the direction of the sun. Finally he said, "OK, you see that big hill over there? Dunkery Beacon?"

"Aye," answered the others eagerly.

"Well, according to the map, we're standing on top of it."

A pair of tourists from Harrogate were out in the fields in Somerset when they discovered an abandoned well near an old farmhouse. Of course they were curious so they dropped a small stone into the well, but they never heard it hit bottom. They searched and found a larger rock and dropped that into the well too. Once again heard nothing. They decided they need something bigger and searched the farmyard for a larger object. They spotted a big wooden railway sleeper and with a lot of effort managed to drag it to the edge of the well and push it over the edge.

After several seconds, a goat tears across the yard and without any hesitation, dives head first into the open hole. The two tourists stand in amazement. Just then a farmer appears and tells them he is looking for a lost goat. The tourists tell the farmer about the goat diving into the well.

"That couldn't be my goat," the farmer replies, "He were tethered in the yard to a blooming great railway sleeper."

During the North East Derby at the Stadium of Light, a 50p piece was thrown onto the pitch during the match; Sunderland's board are still trying to decide if it was a missile or a takeover bid.

A Bolton Wanderers fan phones up the stadium and asks, "What time is kick off?"

"Well," says the manager, "What time can you make it?"

A man from Chorley was visiting his friend in London. They were having tea when the northerner coughed violently, and his false teeth shot across the room and smashed against the wall.

"Oh, dear," he said, "Whatever shall I do? I can't afford a new set."

"Don't worry, mate," said his friend. "I'll get a pair from me sister for you."

The next day the Londoner came back with the teeth, which fitted perfectly.

"This is wonderful," said the northerner. "Your sister must be a very good dentist."

"Oh, she's not a dentist," replied his friend, "she's an undertaker. Waste not want not."

The seven dwarves are down in the mines when there is a cave-in. Snow White runs to the entrance and calls down to them. She hears a faint voice shouting, "Sunderland are going to win the Premier League."

"Well," Snow White says, "at least Dopey's alive!"

Q: What is the difference between Blackburn Rovers and the Bermuda Triangle?
A: The Bermuda triangle has three points.

Q: What do you get when you offer a Sunderland fan a penny for his thoughts?
A: Change!

A man from the fire brigade was conducting a health and safety course at an old people's home in Tyneside.

He asked one old lady, "In the event of a fire, what steps would you take?"

The old lady answered, "Really big ones, ma bonny lad."

On a drive through the Kent orchards, a Brummie noticed a farmer lifting a pig up to an apple tree and holding the pig there as it ate one apple after another.

"Maybe I don't know what I'm talking about," said the Brummie, "but if you just shook the tree so the apples fell to the ground, wouldn't it save a lot of time?"

"Time?" said the farmer, "What does time matter to a pig?"

Q: What did the man from Hull do when he heard that 90% of accidents occur around the home?

A: He moved.

A Geordie was working as a security guard at a big factory on the outskirts of London. He was on duty one day when he spotted a worker walking out of the factory gates pushing a wheelbarrow with a suspicious-looking package in it. The guard stopped the bloke, opened the package up and found it contained nothing but some sawdust and floor-sweepings.

The next day the guard stopped the same worker who was again pushing a wheelbarrow containing a suspicious-looking package. Once again it contained nothing but some sawdust and floor-sweepings.

The same thing happened for several days on the trot. The Geordie was really frustrated – that crafty cockney's up to something, he thought. Finally the guard stopped the worker and said, "OK, I give up. I know you're up to something, man, but I divvint know what."

The worker smirked and said nothing.

"Please, I promise not to turn you in, but put me out of my misery – tell me what you're thieving."

"Alright, mate," laughed the crafty cockney, "I'm stealing wheelbarrows."

In a large stately home in Hampshire, an extremely wealthy man is on his death bed and he calls for his longest serving servants, two locals and a chauffeur from County Durham.

"Chef," he says, "You have been with me for many years and made me some of the nicest meals I've ever had. To you, I shall leave Toff Hall. It has 75 rooms and a large garden. I hope you enjoy it as much as I enjoyed your food."

"Thank you, sir," says Chef and he leaves the room.

The wealthy man turns to his butler.

"Jeeves, you have always been here attending to my every whim at all hours of the day and night for all these years. To you, I shall leave Posh Hall. It has 100 rooms, tennis courts, a large garden and a helipad. I hope it serves you as well as you have served me."

"Thank you, sir," says Jeeves and he leaves the room.

The wealthy man turns to his chauffeur with a grim expression. "And finally you, James, my chauffeur. You, sir, are a disgrace to County Durham. You were never there when I needed you and when you were the car was dirty with empty beer bottles and old cigarette ends all over the interior. I even found some black lace panties on the back seat once. To you, I shall leave damn all."

James nods. "So how many rooms does that one have?" he asks.

A film crew from Glasgow were on location on Bodmin moor. One day an old white-bearded Cornishman went up to the director and said, "Rain tomorrow." The next day it poured.

A week later, the same old local turned up and said to director, "Storm tomorrow."

The next day there was a mighty hailstorm. "That old bloke is absolutely incredible," said the director.

He told his secretary to hire the old man to predict the weather. However, after several successful predictions, the old fellow disappeared. The director was beside himself; the weather was changeable and he was well behind schedule. Finally the director sent a 'runner' out to search for the old man. The 'runner' returned some hours later with the venerable old man in tow.

"I have to shoot a big scene tomorrow," said the director desperately, "and I'm depending on you. What will the weather be like?"

The old Cornishman shrugged his shoulders.
"Don't know," he said. "Radio's broken."

A cockney and his date walk into a very posh furrier in Manchester's Piccadilly.

"Show the lady your finest mink!" orders the cockney.

So the rather snotty shop assistant goes in the back and comes out with an absolutely gorgeous full-length mink coat. As the lady tries it on, the salesman sidles up to the cockney and discreetly whispers, "Ah, sir, that particular fur goes for £65,000." "No problem, mate," says the cockney, "I'll write you a cheque." "Very good, sir," says the smarmy shop assistant, thinking of his commission. "Today is Saturday so you may come by on Monday to pick it up after the bank has cleared the cheque." So the cockney and his very happy date leave the furriers arm-in-arm. On Monday, the cockney returns. The sales assistant is outraged.

"How dare you show your face in here!" he splutters, "There wasn't a single penny in your bank account! Your cheque bounced. You've got a ruddy cheek!"

"Yeah, mate," grinned the cockney, "but I just had to come by to thank you for the best weekend of my life!"

Q: What do you call a Newcastle United fan with an IQ of 10?
A: Supremely gifted!

Q: How do you get them out again?
A: Tell them the rent is due.

A Newcastle girl had just written off her car in a horrific accident on the M1 near London. Miraculously, she managed to pry herself from the wreckage without a scratch and was applying fresh lipstick when a traffic cop arrived.

"Wow!" the officer gasped. "Your car looks like an accordion that was stomped on by an elephant. Are you OK, love?"

"Aye, officer, I'm just canny," the Newcastle girl chirped.

"Well, how in the world did this happen?" the officer asked surveying the wrecked car.

"Officer, it wes the strangest thing!" the Newcastle lass began. "I wes driving alang this road when from oot of nowhere this TREE pops up in front of me. So I swerved to the reet, and there wes another tree! I swerved to the left and there wes ANOTHER tree! I served to the reet and there wes another tree! I swerved to the left and there wes ...."

"Alright, love," the officer said, cutting her off, "There's no trees on the motorway. That was your air freshener swinging back and forth."

Q: How do you get a Wokington family into a post box?
A: Tell them it's a council flat.

A Lancastrian walks into a chip shop in London and says, "Cod and chips twice!" The man behind the counter says, "I heard you the first time."

A man walks into a bar with a dachshund under his arm. The dog is wearing a Sunderland shirt, bobble hat and scarf. The barman says, "Hey! No pets allowed in here. You'll have to leave." The man begs, "Look, I'm desperate. We're both big fans, my TV is broken, and this is the only place we can see the game and it is the Derby."

After securing a promise that the dog will behave and warning that if there is any trouble they will be thrown out, the barman relents and allows them to stay in the bar and watch the game. Sunderland attack from the kick-off and their first goal attempt is cleared off the line for a corner. With that the dog jumps up on the bar and begins walking up and down the bar giving everyone a high-five.

The barman says, "Wow that is the most amazing thing I've ever seen! What does the dog do if they score a goal?"

"I don't know," replies the owner, "I've only had him for four years."

A man from London and a man from Manchester are driving along the A6, one going north and one going south. It's the middle of the night and there are no other cars on the road when they hit each other head on and both cars go flying off in different directions. The Londoner manages to climb out of his car and survey the damage. He looks at his twisted car and says, "Wow, I am really lucky to be alive!"

The Mancunian scrambles out of his car and looks at the wreckage. He too says to himself, "I can't believe I survived this wreck!" The man from Manchester walks over to the man from London and says, "Alright, lad, I think this is a sign that we should live as friends and harbour no hard feelings."

The Londoner thinks for a moment and says, "You know, you're absolutely right. We should be friends. Now I'm gonna see what else survived the wreck."

So he pops open his boot and finds a bottle of brandy. He says to the Mancunian, "You know what, mate? I think this is another sign and we should toast to our new-found understanding and friendship."

The Mancunian says, "You're dead right!" and he grabs the bottle and starts swigging down the brandy. After putting away nearly half the bottle, the Mancunian hands it back to the Londoner and says, "Your turn!"

The Londoner twists the cap back on the bottle and says, "Nahh, I think I'll wait for the police to show up."

A little girl gets lost in a big shopping centre in Gateshead. She wanders around for a while then asks one of the security guards to help her find her mummy. The security guard says to her, "What's your mum like?"

"Fags and vodka," says the little girl.

A not so pretty girl from Workington goes to a posh beauty salon in London.

"I'm sorry, dear," says the receptionist, "This is a beauticians not a magicians!"

Two businessmen were admiring their new shop in Edinburgh's Royal Mile. It wasn't quite ready with only a few shelves set up.

One said to the other, "I bet any minute now some thick tourist is going to walk by, put his face to the window and ask what we're selling."

No sooner were the words out of his mouth when, sure enough, a curious Londoner walked to the window, had a peek, and in a broad cockney accent asked "What you sellin' 'ere, mate?"

"We're selling dingbats," replied one of the Scots sarcastically. Without skipping a beat, the Londoner said, "Yer doing well then ... Only two left!"

Alice dies, aged 78, having attended church in Bolton every Sunday of her life. Her husband, Joe, asks the stonemason for a headstone with the words: *Lord, she was thine.*

A week later Joe returns to the stonemason to find that he has engraved: *Lord she was thin.*

Joe says, "You've missed off the 'e', you'll have to do it again."

Another week passes and Joe goes to see the stone on the grave; it now reads: *Ee Lord she was thin.*

Ten women out on a hen night in Newcastle thought it would be sensible if one of them stayed more sober than the other nine and looked after the money to pay for their drinks. After deciding who would hold the money, they all put twenty pounds into the kitty to cover expenses. At closing time after a few beers, some jello shots, several vodka and cokes, and a Pina Colada each, they stood around deciding how to divvy up the leftover cash.

"How do we stand?" said Sharon.

"Stand?!" said Debbie. "That's the easy part! I'm wondering how I can walk. I've missed the last bus to Cowgate!"

At a barracks near Salisbury Plain, the Sergeant Major asks the new recruits on parade, "Does anybody here know the difference between a bread roll and a rock?"

"I do, sir!" says an eager young squaddie from Stafford putting his hand up.

"Good," says the Sergeant Major, "You're cooking breakfast."

A Scouser walks into a bar in London and decides to wind up the barman.

"Gizza a packet of helicopter crisps, whack," he says.

"I'm sorry," the barman replies, without missing a beat, "We only have plane."

A Londoner walks into a bar in Liverpool with his pit bull terrier.

"You can't bring that dog in here, whack," says the barman.

The dog seems to understand, leaps over the bar, knocks off the barman's cap and eats it.

"Get out!" the angry barman says to the Londoner, "And take that dog with yous. I don't like yer attitude."

"It wasn't me 'at 'e chewed, mate," says the Londoner, "it was yourn."

A Yorkshire man arrived rather late at night at a B&B in Southend where he had made a reservation. The place was in darkness, so he knocked loudly on the door. After a long time a light appeared in an upstairs window and a woman in curlers stuck her head out, "Who are you?" she shouted bad-temperedly. "What do you want at this blooming time of night?"

"I'm staying here!" called the Yorkshire man.

"Stay there, then," retorted the landlady and she slammed the window shut.

A Carlisle man on holiday visited a tiny village on the Cornish coast. On the quay a local fisherman was selling his catch. The tourist complimented him on the quality of his fish and asked how long it took him to catch them.

"Not very long, me boy," answered the fisherman.

"But then, why didn't you stay out longer and catch more?" asked the tourist.

The Cornishman explained that his small catch was sufficient to meet his needs and those of his family.

The tourist asked, "So what do you do with the rest of your time?"

"Oi sleep late, fish a little, play with me children, spend time with me missus," said the fisherman, "In the evenings oi nip into the village to see the boys, 'ave a few pints, play darts, chat up barmaids, and sing a few songs. On Saturdays oi watch footie and Sundays I play cricket. Oi 'ave a lovely life."

"I have a M.B.A. from the Carlisle School of Business and I can help you," said the tourist, "You should start by fishing longer every day. You can then sell the extra fish you catch. With the extra revenue, you can buy a bigger boat. With the extra money the larger boat will bring, you can buy a second one and a third one and so on until you have an entire fleet of trawlers. Instead of selling your fish to a middleman, you can negotiate directly with the processing plants and maybe even open your own plant. You can then leave this little village and move to Leeds, York, or even London! From there you can direct your huge enterprise."

"How long would that take, me 'andsome?" asked the Cornishman.

"Twenty, perhaps twenty-five years," replied the tourist.
"And after that?" asked the Cornishman.

"Afterwards? That's when it gets really interesting," answered the tourist, laughing. "When your business gets really big, you can start selling stocks and make millions!"

"Millions? Really?" asked the Cornishman. "And after that?"
"After that," the tourist replied, "you'll be able to retire, live in a tiny village near the coast, sleep late, play with your children, catch a few fish, spend time with your wife, spend your evenings drinking and hanging out with your friends…"

A tourist from Edinburgh, loaded with expensive fishing rods and equipment, approaches an old fisherman sitting on the bank of the River Exe in Devon.

"I say, old man," says the Edinburgh man, "Is this river any good for fish?"

"It must be," said the old Devonian, "Oi can't get none of 'em to leave it."

A Geordie was showing off to his friend, "I had a meal oot last neet. I ordered everything in French, surprised everybody. It was a Chinese restaurant."

Simon was down on his luck so he thought he would try getting a few odd jobs by calling at the posh houses in Wynyard in the Tees Valley. After a few "no ways", a guy in one of the big houses thought he would give him a break and says, "The porch needs painting so I'll give you £50 to paint it for me."

"You're a life-saver, mister," says Simon, "Arl dee it reet away!" Time passes until…

"There yer go, Ah'm all done with the painting."

"Well, here's your £50," says the homeowner, handing over some crisp tenners.

"Thanks very much," says Simon, pocketing the money, "Oh and by the way, it's a Ferrari, not a Porsche!"

One freezing cold December day, two blondes went for a walk in Sherwood Forest in search of the perfect Christmas tree. Finally, after five hours looking, one turns to the other and says crossly, "That's it, I've had enough. I'm chopping down the next fir tree we see, whether it's decorated or not!"

An ex-traffic warden walks into a pizzeria in Sheffield and orders a pizza.

The waiter asks him, "Should I cut it into six pieces or eight pieces?"

The ex-traffic warden replies, "I'm feeling right hungry, lad. You'd better cut it into eight pieces."

A cockney and a Geordie are walking along the beach at South Shields when the Londoner kicks a tin pot in the sand. Picking it up he starts to clean it and with a flash and a roll of thunder out pops a genie.

"Oh thank you, master. I have been trapped in that pot for ten thousand years. What is your command?"

The jealous Geordie says, "Hang on a minute, man, we're together surely we both get a wish?"

"As my cockney master commands," says the genie.

"OK," says the Londoner, "give the bloke a wish."

"Right," says the Geordie, "I want a high wall built right around the city of Newcastle to keep all those soft southern so-and-sos out. It must be twice as high as the tallest man, and strong, no weaknesses at all."

"Your wish is my command," says the genie, "now my cockney master, what is your wish?"

"Let's get this clear, mate," says the Londoner, "a high wall, right around the city, no weaknesses, no windows, no doors, no gates, solid?"

"That's right, " says the Geordie, "Now what about your wish?"
"Easy," says the cockney, "Fill it with water!"

A newspaper boy was standing on the corner of a London street with a stack of papers, yelling, "Read all about it. Fifty people swindled! Fifty people swindled!"

Curious, a tourist from Kendal walked over, bought a paper, and checked the front page. Finding nothing, the Cumbrian said indignantly, "There's nowt in here about fifty people being swindled, lad."

The newspaper boy ignored him and went on, calling out, "Read all about it. Fifty-one people swindled!"

A northerner goes south to the New Forest to be a lumberjack. On his first day on the job, the boss gives him a chainsaw and says, "Listen, chum, I expect one hundred trees felled per day, if you don't make the grade you're out!"

Twelve hours later, the northerner staggers back into the camp and collapses.

"How many trees, mate?" asks the boss.

"Ninety-seven," croaks the filthy, exhausted northerner.
The boss sees how pathetic he looks and gives him one last chance.

Next day, after thirteen hours the northerner is carried in by the other forestry workers.

"How many?" says the boss.

"Ninety-eight," says the sweaty, breathless northerner.

Another lumberjack says, "Hey boss, that northerner might be a sad specimen, but he worked non-stop for thirteen hours, no lunch, nothing!"

The boss wonders if the northerner's chainsaw might be faulty so he pulls the cord. The saw roars into life. The northerner leaps up and shouts, "Blooming heck! What's

A shy young man from Somerset visits Manchester for the weekend and goes into a smart cocktail lounge. He spots a beautiful woman sitting at the bar. After an hour of gathering up his courage, he finally goes over to her and asks tentatively, "Would you mind if I chatted to you for a while?"

The beautiful woman looks at him disdainfully and yells at the top of her voice, "NO, I WON'T GO BACK TO YOUR HOTEL WITH YOU TONIGHT!!"

Everyone in the bar is now staring at them. Naturally, the young man from Somerset is hopelessly embarrassed. He slinks back to his table feeling like a real country bumpkin. After a few minutes, the beautiful woman walks over to him and smiles at him apologetically.

"I'm sorry if I embarrassed you," she says, "You see, I'm a journalist and I've got an assignment to study how people respond to embarrassing situations."

"That's OK," says the young man from Somerset, then he takes a deep breath and shouts as loud as he can, "WHAT DO YOU MEAN £200?!!?"

Q: What's the first question at a Liverpudlian quiz night?
A: 'What you lookin' at?'

After a night on the town, two Geordie girls lock the keys in their BMW. One of the girls tries to break into the car while the other one takes pictures on her phone.

Finally the first Geordie girl says, "Howay, man! Sta taking pics, Linda, an' try an' help, I cannit git intee this car!"

"Keep tryin', pet," says her friend, "Hurry up – it looks leek it's ganing tuh rain an' the top's doon."

A Yorkshire couple go to the Costa Brava for a self-catering holiday, but on arrival, the wife says, "I won't be able to make gravy with your dinner, love – I've forgotten the Bisto."

The husband says, "Don't worry, there's a couple from down south staying in the next apartment, I'll see if they have any." So he knocks on the door of the next apartment, and says to the man, "'Allo, hast any Bisto?"

"Jog off, amigo!" says the southerner slamming the door, "No hablo Espanol."

A general inspecting troops in Hampshire ordered the parade to don gas masks. He paused opposite a northern soldier. Pointing to the eyepiece of his respirator, he inquired, "Soldier, where is your anti-mist?"

"Don't know, sir," came the reply, "Reckon she's oop with Uncle Albert in Oldham."

A Kentish man, a Londoner and a Yorkshire man were sitting talking in the pub. The two southerners were talking about who wore the trousers in their households.

The Kentish man said, "I love my wife so I let her make all the decisions."

The Londoner said, "Yeah, me an' me missus share everything." "More fool you," said the Yorkshire man, "I'm gaffer in ma 'ouse." "Is that right, mate?" asked the Kentish man.

"You control yer missus, d'ya?" asked the Londoner.

"Aye, 'appen I do, lad," boasted the Yorkshire man, "Only t' other night ma missus came to me on her hands and knees."
The southerners were amazed. "What happened then?" they asked.

The Yorkshire man replied, "She said, 'Get out from under the bed and fight like a man'."